An American Rodeo
Riding and Roping

Lisa Gabbert

The Rosen Publishing Group's
PowerKids Press ™
New York

To Dad, with love.

Published in 1999 by The Rosen Publishing Group, Inc.
29 East 21st Street, New York, NY 10010

First Edition

Book Design: Michael de Guzman

Photo Credits: p. 4 © Warren Faidley/International Stock; pp. 7, 8, 11, 12, 15, 16 © Joe Viesti/Viesti Associates, Inc.; p. 19 © Martha Cooper/Viesti Associates, Inc.; p. 20 © Mike Lichter/International Stock.

Gabbert, Lisa.
    An American rodeo: riding and roping / Lisa Gabbert.
        p.   cm. — (Festivals! USA)
    Includes index.
    Summary: Describes the work that cowboys do and how events at a rodeo evolved as a test of cowboys' skills.
    ISBN 0-8239-5339-4
    1. Rodeos—United States—Juvenile literature. [1. Rodeos. 2. Cowboys.]
    I. Title. II. Series.
GV1834.5.G33 1998
791.8'4'0973—dc21

                                                98-6474
                                                   CIP
                                                       AC

Manufactured in the United States of America

Contents

1 What Is a Rodeo? 5

2 Cowboys 6

3 Rodeos and Ranch Life 9

4 When Was the First Rodeo? 10

5 Rodeos and Wild West Shows 13

6 Bucking Broncos 14

7 Barrel Racing 17

8 Bull Riding 18

9 Rodeo Clowns 21

10 A Part of History 22

Glossary 23

Index 24

What Is a Rodeo?

A **rodeo** (ROH-dee-oh) is both a cowboy contest and a **professional** (pro-FEH-shuh-nul) sport. **Contestants** (kun-TES-tunts) compete against each other to win prize money. Rodeos are usually held in the summer, especially around the Fourth of July. There are hundreds of rodeos in the United States. Rodeos can be called by other names too, such as the Cheyenne Frontier Days in Wyoming, the Calgary Stampede in Canada, and the Pendleton Roundup in Oregon.

During rodeos, cowboys show how good they are at their jobs.

Cowboys

The word for cowboy in Spanish is ***vaquero*** (bah-KAYR-oh), which became **buckaroo** (buk-uh-ROO) in English. Cowboys are still called buckaroos in some places in the United States. A cowboy works on a ranch and rides on a horse while he herds cattle. Cowboys sometimes compete in small, local rodeos. In large rodeos, many rodeo contestants are professional athletes who compete all over the country.

A cowboy may spend an entire day on horseback when he's herding cattle. ▶

Rodeos and Ranch Life

Cowboys develop special skills as they work with cattle on big ranches. These skills include roping, **lassoing** (LASS-oh-ing), and riding styles. Cowboys have contests among themselves to test these special skills. Sometimes large ranches compete as teams against other ranches. These contests became known as rodeos. Other events, such as bull riding, have become a part of rodeos today.

Although it may look scary, calves aren't hurt in roping contests.

When Was the First Rodeo?

Nobody really knows about the first rodeo. Many people think that rodeos began in the western United States, but they probably developed from the Mexican rodeo, or **charreada** (char-ee-AH-dah). *Charreadas* were brought to Mexico by **conquistadors** (kon-KEES-tah-dorz) from Spain. The conquistadors wanted to show off their skills with horses and bulls. For many years during the 1800s, rodeos and *charreadas* in the southwestern United States were similar.

A charreada has many of the same events as a rodeo. ▶

Rodeos and Wild West Shows

Buffalo Bill was a **frontiersman** (frun-TEERZ-man) who opened a Wild West Show in 1883. Buffalo Bill's Wild West show traveled across the world and became very famous. It **staged** (STAYJD) Indian fights, stagecoach robberies, and hired cowboys and cowgirls to wrestle bulls, ride horses, and perform trick roping. For some people, the Wild West Show was the only time they would ever see a cowboy.

Buffalo Bill's Wild West Show closed after World War I, but Buffalo Bill had helped start an American tradition.

Bucking Broncos

A **bucking bronco** (BUK-ing BRON-koh) is a horse that tries to throw the rider off its back by jumping and kicking. Riding bucking broncos is a popular event in rodeos and used to be part of a cowboy's job on a ranch. Cowboys **tamed** (TAYMD) young, wild horses by riding them until the horse stopped bucking. These men were called "bronco busters." Today, rodeo contestants ride bucking broncos for eight seconds.

Cowboys can ride with a saddle or without one, which is called bareback.

Cowboys are timed to see how long they can stay on a bucking bronco.

15

Barrel Racing

Barrel racing is another rodeo event. Contestants enter an empty **corral** (kor-AL) on horseback, racing at full speed. The riders race their horses around barrels in a pattern that looks like a clover leaf. They try to come as close as possible to the barrels without tipping them over. In barrel racing, contestants race against each other to see who is the fastest. Although women compete in other events, barrel racing is the only all-women event.

◀ *Teamwork between the rider and horse is important in barrel racing.*

Bull Riding

Bull riding is the most dangerous rodeo event. Bulls can weigh more than 2,000 pounds and are very fast. To ride a bull, a cowboy holds tight onto a rope that is looped around a bull's chest. The cowboy must be very careful not to get caught on the bull's horns! The bull tries to buck the rider off his back. The cowboy tries to stay on the bull for as long as he can without falling off. When he falls, the cowboy must quickly get out of the bull's way so he doesn't get hurt.

It takes a lot of training and patience to become a successful bull rider. ▶

Rodeo Clowns

Rodeo clowns are very good athletes. Some rodeo clowns are funny and work with animals such as trained dogs. Other clowns are an important part of the bull-riding event. They distract the bull when the cowboy falls off it. Some clowns make the bulls run after them. Then they hide inside barrels made especially for the clowns. The best barrels are made from special **material** (muh-TEER-ee-uhl) that can handle a bull's horns. Other clowns distract the bull by waving flags.

Rodeo clowns help riders get to safety, but they have to think and act quickly or they could get hurt too.

A Part of History

Today, the rodeo is an important part of American **culture** (KUL-cher). Whole families can take part in a rodeo, and family and friends support one another in each event. The rodeo is a time for people to come together for fun, but it is also a time to remember and respect the history of the Wild West.

There may be a rodeo happening near you!

Cheyenne Frontier Days, Cheyenne, WY   (800) 227-6336
Grand National Rodeo, San Francisco, CA (415) 469-6065
National Finals Rodeo, Las Vegas, NV   (702) 731-2115

Glossary

buckaroo (buk-uh-ROO) A cowboy.

bucking bronco (BUK-ing BRON-koh) A horse that jumps and kicks its hind legs to throw off the rider.

charreada (char-ee-AH-dah) A Mexican rodeo.

conquistador (kon-KEES-tah-dor) A Spanish explorer.

contestant (kun-TES-tunt) A person competing in a contest.

corral (kor-AL) A pen for holding horses or other animals.

culture (KUL-cher) The beliefs, customs, art, and religions of a group of people.

frontiersman (frun-TEERZ-man) Someone who lives and works in an area that hasn't yet been settled.

lasso (LASS-oh) To capture something with a rope.

material (muh-TEER-ee-uhl) What something is made of or used for.

professional (pro-FEH-shuh-nul) To be paid for playing a sport.

rodeo (ROH-dee-oh) A contest where a person's skills in roping cattle and riding horses is tested against others.

stage (STAYJ) To act out.

tame (TAYM) To make calm.

vaquero (bah-KAYR-oh) The Spanish word for cowboy.

Index

B
barrel racing, 17
buckaroo, 6
bucking bronco, 14
Buffalo Bill, 13
Buffalo Bill's Wild West Show, 13
bull riding, 9, 18, 21

C
cattle, 6, 9
charreada, 10
conquistadors, 10
contest, 5, 9

contestant, 5, 6, 14, 17
corral, 17
cowboys, 5, 6, 9, 13, 14, 15, 18, 21
culture, 22

F
frontiersman, 13

L
lassoing, 9

M
material, 21

P
professional, 5, 6

R
ranches, 6, 9, 14
rodeo clowns, 21
roping, 9

S
saddle, 15
stage, 13

T
tame, 14

V
vaquero, 6